IN THE NAME OF GOD

The Marigolds Island

Written by Asadollah Tavakoli

Edited Soroush Melatparast

Illustrated by Amirhossein Asadi

Designed by Farzaneh Karkevandi

Publishing:Taraneh Pedram

ISBN 9786008881612

T.Pedrampub.
00989308874407

The Marigolds Island

By: Asadollah Tavakoli

Imagine a beautiful island in the heart of a big ocean. We call it "Marigold Island".

In addition to very old trees which express the stories from the past of the island, like coming into existence & appearance, I narrate you some attractive & honeyed stories.

Beautiful flowers live all together or in some places, they live with other kinds of flowers. For all that beauties, passions & liveliness, no bird or animal live there.

Recently, a nightingale has decided to come to & live in this calm & secluded place. Thinking for long, he is going to plant a bud of a tree on which make a nest for himself & enjoy all these beautiful flowers & their sweet smell. Here, we start the story:

Contents

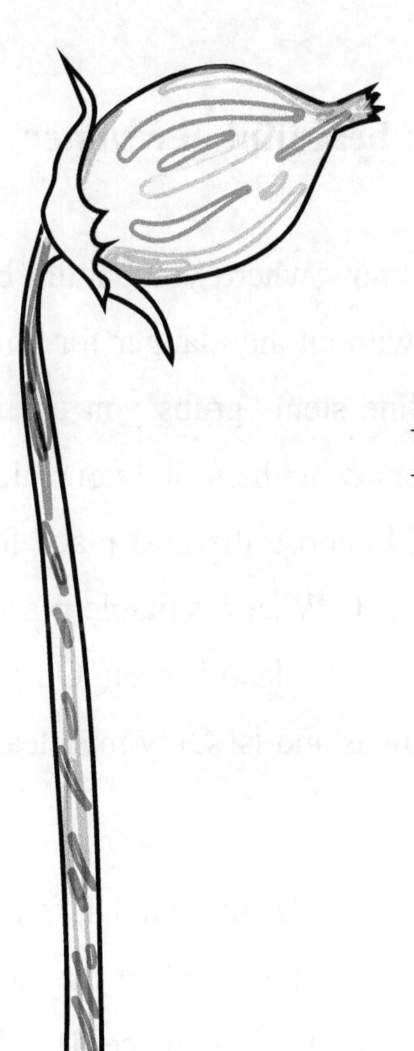

Part 1

The nightingale: beautiful newcomer

– My dear sapling, I know where you should be planted. A safe place without any danger for you. Never your roots & fine stems grubs you up by storms & beachcombers & withers like your nice mother. Right. I should choose the best place for you. Lalalalalala… Got it! What a suitable place! From this point, all over the island is seen. Oh my God! How beautiful this island is! Only my pleasant song is missed.

It's like the lofty paradise. Thanks God I found this safe place. Yeah! It's better to plant the sapling by the spring, yes! It's the best place. Beside the native common poppies of that region. What various colors, red, purple, yellow, white. Oh my

God! Where is the best place? Everywhere I want to plant it, it seems wrong. Because everywhere is not suitable for it. God's domination on the devil! Why this much of temptation? Go, leave me alone. Here, by the spring is the best. My dear! My God sapling! I'm afraid you. Whiter till I find a place for you. Be ready my love. What a limped water. Drink how much you want to grow your beautiful branches. I try to be next to you. Forever provided that you grow up soon, when you grow up, my wife & I will live with you. Stay besides this beautiful flower, so that I prepare your roots bed. Oh, I forgot to taste the water whether it's sweet or not. My flower should drink sweet water. I meet all tour needs to be glad with you, what a refreshing water! Oh! I find the place. I should dig here and plant you in the soil. The nightingale put the sapling inside the hole and filled it out with soft soil. He went far and watched it. He thought" you great. La La La ….He dived into the water.

Swimming of great for me. I'm not tried anymore. The nightingale went back. Gaily.

Hey Marigold flowers! Goodbye. Wait for me. See you soon dear.

Two months later

Dandelion: Oh! What a fine morning. Wake up common poppies. The sun is about to show herself. Get up and wash your face. Now, breeze starts to blow. The morning dance is beginning. Hurry up! Dear ipomoea be ready. Let's dance. Hurry up. Dear common poppy! Don't be naughty. Where are you looking at? Be happy with this morning sports called" dance". Dear Ipomoea! Look at here. Where is your mind?" Dear common poppy! Look at there. A newcomer! What a beautiful one. Look."

All the flowers look at the side which the ipomoea pointed and dance together. Common poppy says surprisingly:" what a beautiful flower. I've never seen such a nice one. Don't be noisy. One of us as our agent should talk to and know her better and introduce her. You, chrysanthemums!

Are you ready to do this?

Chrysanthemums No! No! That's not my job. She ravishes all hearts. So that I loose myself. It's better to do this white common poppy."

Ipomoea:" Dear common poppy! You do it. I don't think you are shy like this Chrysanthemums .Common poppy happily accepts: thank you for entrusting it to me. Ipomoea thanks white common poopy:" I'm glad that white common poppy goes in for everything."

Bravo- sweet heart.

White Poppies shouts excitedly: "the honor is mine.
Wait a moment. Let me tidy up myself. We should
be polite with this beautiful new camera.

She tells Chrysanthemums "dear! Remember not
to entrust your job to another one". Oh! My God!
Look! All the flowers wonder. What a nice figure.
What a beautiful creation. Oh, my God! I want to
talk to her. Sooner and be here friend. I think her
talking is as nice as her stems. Apparently she has
a lovely voice and attractive words the newcomer:

I don't understand what's happening. Why everybody looking at me? Have they seen such flower
yet? I'm not wrong. Right!

All are watching me. They're right. Because I'm not from here. That red flower is much beautiful. One of white poppies is coming to me. What a graceful walking. What a figure! Someone calls me. She calls the newcomer! Lively, hey newcomer! Why don't you answer me?

Sorry white Poppy! Are you with me?

White poppies smiles and reaches in two steps and embraces her.

"How you are beautiful and lovely. How you ravish, few flowers are like you with this little figure. Lady like and dignified.

White poppies: forgot to say hello. Welcome to our Island. May you introduce yourself? Where are from? The newcomer: "hello sweet heart. In this beautiful morning, I am full of happiness because of visiting my kind friends, here is so crowded.

The white poppies: good morning. You who are the most beautiful, all of us are proud of such flower.

The newcomer: " good morning everybody. You are all nice/ coy. If God has given you both beauty and kind hearts. Here, it is worth thanking God for everything. I hope to have nice days together."

White poppies would you introduce yourself? All of my friends want to get familiar with you. Do us a favor. ?"

Lilies watches the newcomer's behavior and says: in addition to have an excellent figure, her voice charms us. Well done."

Dandelion: "Don't speak listen to her. All the island's habitants became aware of her by my people.

We should see how she behaves and says. What a dreamy morning.”

Lilies: enough Dandelion! I just said something. Leave it. Then you suggest me not to speak. “

Dandelion: excuse me I bother you, ok dear lilies.

The newcomer” wow! I should introduce myself first. Excuse me all nice flowers. As my appearance shows, I’m known as “seven-colored flower”.

That’s the name of our family. It was our family name in the island where my mother lived. I have a food name dear anemone. Does it suit me or not?

All flowers loudly:” seven- colored flower.” It does suit you.”

Lilies: It’s an excellent choice. Bravo.

Seven- colored flower: "thank you all. You all favor me. May I be one of you?" The bud:" Well, you are of us. I mean, we have no choice/ option. You are a resident of this island."

The red anemone: what do you mean? She is a member of our family. Did you listen my dear? It is better to watch only."

The bud:" I meant nothing. Sorry. "

The Chrysanthemums: no one told you have bad intension. Don't worry."

The lilies: but never disrupt adults' speech. It's good that you understand it dear bud."

The bud:" I promise not to speak, but when someone asks me."

All of the flowers: "Bravo our dear bud."

Lilies my dear friends! Listen! Listen! {All become quite}. Marigold! Don't' you tell anything? "

Marigold: "I have few word. Whatever is need, you said but I think I should become more familiar with you and our environment. Of course I have many things to say and I will tell you all of my memories during these future days."

The Anemone" we should be patient and wait for your sweet words"

Seven-colored flower" oh my dears.   Oh my dears. I will willingly tell you where I come from. I think my memories are interesting. Are you agreed?"

All of the flowers: "this is our request. We are en-thusiastically ready to listen to your words."

Seven colored flower: So everybody look! First I

read a poem, then I'll go on:

God knows of creation, who runs the world

The time lapse are all memories, I want to tell a story of mine & the world

Here, we all are being, we all are of God

We all thank & call you, we need your favor

The flowers city is your miracle, everyone praises you forever

Tulip: "Bravo seven-colored flower." Whatever you say is our own words. All of us are happy and honor to have such friend.

Seven-colored flower: thank you all. Now I tell the memory that you all, my friends, will to know:

There's a beautiful island near this island. But there's not much of distance. It has good and fresh weather, too. Many old and tall trees live there which we don't have them in this island or only we see their survivals.

Its blue sky, golden sunlight, beautiful evening, moonlight and stars have special beauty. My dear mother who I'm a sapling of her grew up and became huge. According to the habitants of that island, my mother is the sample of beauty. What a good time. Of course I heard these words from a nice bird who brought me here. She got sick that I'll tell about it later. I grew up in our island and now I'm here and enjoy living close to you.

Days and years passed till my mother, that nice tree, became sick.

Birds found my mother's leaves turn yellow. They asked about it. She answered:" my roots were eradicated by the waves of the sea. Because I live by the sea and I feel the annihilation danger. So I asked birds to plant the sapling of mine in a safe place, in order to survive my generation. At last I will dry and wither." Only there is a beautiful nightingale cut the sapling of her and brought to this island. I am the fruit of that transplantation. So that, I will be far from that stormy waves. That beautiful melodies bird comes to me and lands on my fine stems. And we talk about the past and present every day. Yesterday, he said that my mother is still alive and flaunting. Because the water of the sea has come down a little and harms her roots less. Now I'm so glad that I walk on air. The nightingales decided to send me two of their polts. Wonderful! They are good and loyal friends.

Right. Now it's the time that bird appears. He has a nice voice, if he comes I ask him sing."

Flowers:" sure! Ask him to sing. We love beauties.

The nightingale: Hey My beautiful flower! I come today, you are in a good mood. You are busy. What's happen?"

Seven-colored flower: yes, they're my friends. Why are you late?

The nightingale: "because my chickens were exercising to fly. I should have token care of and feed them. Cause they've grown a lot. They need more food. Hahaha… why are you tickling me? You make me laugh. It's not good."

The seven-colored flower: "I'm fondling you. I'm perfuming your feathers with my smell. Oh! You seem so tired. I want to rest up your tiredness. Don't you like?"

The nightingale: "Because that sharp stem is going into my eye. By the way, your mother sends the regards. I told her about your beauties. She became so happy. According to her order, I planted her two other saplings in two points of this island. It was her request, but none of them is as beautiful as you."

The seven-colored flower: "Oh sorry my friends! This naughty nightingale distracted me completely. I ask him to sing a song, instead. Dear nightingale! Don't keep them waiting."

The nightingale: "Sweet-heart! What should I sing? Wait a moment."

The seven-colored flower: "You made me so tired. Why don't you sing? Everybody's waiting. Sing for my friends & me.”

-Lalalalala…

The nightingale: “Ok! Why are you in hurry?”

All of the flowers: “We all love you. Lalalalala...”

The nightingale: “Wait. I think about what I want to sing. Hey! You started before me. Look! Everybody’s dancing. Oh! What a funny time! What I’m waiting for! I should go along with them. I’m falling behind.”

Swear on love & frenzy!

Swear on passion & happiness,

Swear on flowers’ spirit

The nightingales’ melody,

We all are of God

Reminding happiness, the cheerful dance of flowers'

The nightingales' melody,

All the flowers laughing

Hyacinths' dance, the nightingales' melody,

Swear on love & frenzy!

Swear on passion & happiness,

Swear on flowers' spirit

The nightingales' melody,

The nightingale: "Well, it's late. I should go. My
seven-colored flower & my beautiful flowers!
Goodbye & see you tomorrow."

The seven-colored flower: "Goodbye. Come back soon tomorrow. We'll miss you."

The tulip: "Friends! Listen. Let's sing a song together, but which one?"

The clove: "Friendship song."

The Anemone: "What are you waiting for? Star."

The nightingale: "What a clamor! It's interesting to see them. Wish you all happy moments. Be friends forever. Be safe from any badness. Goodbye beauties."

End of part newcomer.

Part 2

The Lilac

The two birds mentioned in the first part, are excursing in Marigold Island. They proud themselves on flowers having fragrant smell. The two birds are making love, flying cheerfully to the other side of the island & watching whatever are on the ground. They are excitedly singing & landing on the flower. One of them starts singing involuntarily:

O'God! You please the flowers, I'm astonished by your synthesis,

Every flower glows of randan and love

The flower on which the nightingale sits, peeks him. Then, says charmingly: "You! Little bird!

What's your name? In which school of nature you learned love & delight?"

The nightingale becomes silent for a moment, but he tends to answer, opens his mouth & sings:

Oh! The puzzled nightingale of my plain

Lost the love in this plain

God created all of us, us & you

It is ours to sight these charms

The flower who lost her heart, because of the nightingale's fluent words, says: "that's right that God has created us. I tell you after all of these rhythmic & charming words, because this is full of goodness & specially God's favor. Yes. Tell! I have never heard such fluent words. Recite about God's kindness & mercy which we all need."

The nightingale waits a moment & reviews the beautiful flower's words, looks at his wife who was still perfuming herself with the flower's perfume. He looks at the flower & says: "But you, beautiful flower, didn't say anything about yourself. Isn't better to open your mouth, say sweet words & whatever you want?"

The flower smiles & says: "I'm the lilac. This kind of flowers are found in different colors, such as white, lilac color, etc. most of the flowers of this island live long. For example I'm ten years old. I wish to live for many years. As you know, here is always spring, but sometimes flowers & plants wither after the pollination gradually & then, their seeds start to grow, like that bean flower that produced the seeds & then withered. But after a few weeks, it spread the seeds, grew again & survived. All of God's wonders, miracles & creatures are seen everywhere. You should stay here for a long time to become aware."

The sound of flying of the nightingale's partner is heard. She sits on the lilac fascinatingly & says: "Hello. Here is full of different & fragrant smells that I wonder which one to use for perfuming! We have lots of words to express for the habitants of the island. Dear lilac! I'll come to see you again. Wait for us. Goodbye my dears."

We stay with you

we became two plagued lovers, companion of wine

I do not leave you I stay with you to be ecstatic Where this much frenzy,

we became ravishment of sweetheart

Everywhere in the nature is luxury

may you enjoy it we became wise

Here is luxury shore, dear

wait, we became shining

Before us flower garment has opened

became dear lovers' lane

Garden is our house lawn

by our eyes we became shining

Kiss my chick, lip to lip resident of tavern we
became frenzied with love

All frenzied with lover creator

we remained to be shielding

Part 3

Climbing Rose

It's a beautiful & pleasurable morning. The good-smell flower ravishes. The nightingale is singing & flying from one branch to another. The habitants of the island are observing his beautiful show & enjoying it. The nightingale sings:

Oh my God you are deserved greatness oh my God you are deserve Divinity

Such you create omnifarious flowers which painters were wondered because of His creative power

Lawn bride with heart- stealing

gives happiness to sprit

If I do not praise you every time and do not praise your favor

My tongue should be cut or we all should resign ourselves to the will of Gods

Suddenly, that song brings back the nightingale to himself & he says: "My dear wife! Don't you want to go anywhere today?"

The seven-colored flower objects: "Why do you leave me every day?"

The father nightingale answers: "Dear seven-colored flower! Our leaving for a moment or a day doesn't mean that we want to leave you. Everybody should travel to read, to learn & to know. We should be aware of every flower's secret. We should have new words & news to talk about every day. Am not right?"

The seven-colored flower: "I'm afraid of missing you or someone else comes to your heart & then you leave me."

Now, the seven-colored flower's tears drop down.

The father nightingale: "Anywhere I be, my heart belongs to God, first & then to you. I never leave you. You lacerated my heart. Don't cry. Your tears are pure. I don't sewer, but you are of me & I'm of you."

She says cheerfully & laughingly: "I knew it. My dear! I don't know why I became upset. I couldn't help it."

The nightingale: "know that the promise between the flower & the nightingale is unbreakable & it has its special secret which is unspeakable."

The seven-colored flower feels assured & says: "Whatever needs, I knew & I found it that the real lovers may not separate. Everywhere they are, they don't leave their love. Our pleasure divine, I worth your requests &I'm created for the very true way."

A voice attracts their attention: "You agile bird! Join us to talk about everything, to prostrate our creator, to praise God who creates beauties specially this good-voiced bird to know love & speak kindly, maybe we seek the favor of God."

The lover nightingale who heard these fluent words ravishes, he joins the holder's voice as rapid as possible as a stone left its sling, then, becomes calm, invites his wife, talks with the flowers who called him to find that flowers want to entertain him, a flower who is bigger than rose, full of big red flowers from the ground to the top.

The beautiful flower: "First I introduce myself. I'm climbing rose. Welcome to the Marigold Island."

The father & mother nightingale look at each other. The father nightingale unpassionately says: "What the almighty God has given you is a great blessing. Have you ever praised your God?"

The climbing rose says smilingly & surprisingly: "When I was born, I knew God. He brought up us & he met everything we need. We thank God, the creator of the world who is rich. This is our way. Thus, God gave us the beauty. We have experienced his kindness before."

The nightingale says embarrassingly: "Pardon me that I told you that way. I stammer…"

The rose: "Actually, you did the right thing. This is the Greats' way that they tell their words clearly & express their opinion obviously."

The nightingale says unhappily: "O'God! Is there anybody who don't thank you? Whether you create friends such beautiful, open their tongue & astonish their eyes, whereas they prostrate you! God! You deserve the greatness."

Immediately, the flowers, the rose & the nightingales look at each other & recite the ((Thanks Song)).

O'God thanks a lot for creation that gave us body, spirit and thought

Niceness is seen everywhere we step

thousands thousands blessing we see

O' my God you are thankers' refuge

it is not divine route but you

All your attendance in this Island

cause everybody rules over ones' desire

If you want paradise in futurity

Ask God prosperity all the time

Don't disobey God's order

Don't turn your face from God

Among a nice uproar, the nightingale thanks everybody & says: "Whatever we saw & see in the future, makes us more serious to obey. I thank all the flowers, specially the climbing rose & hope that I can say my praise. Goodbye my dear friends because of our wonderful entertaining."

I go to pass with nature

pass my kindness with flower garden

Everywhere I'm fine and heart- stealing   love and
happiness cause of joie de vivre and purity

Whatever I see is greatness and beautiful Steal in-
telligent loyal kindness

Sweet heart group group

charm charm take us walking proudly into both
worlds

Give sadness take joy fearless I say with you play
reed

I go to pass the night

this nature set up exciting

Goodbye that I went I praise God

Now, the seven-colored flower, who is happier than before, is talking with beautiful birds. She says: "Dear nightingale! You planted me in the best place of the island. I can see anything to the far island. I felt many times that all of the habitants of the is-land can see & praise me. Look! Every flowers are just one-colored, like red, white, pink, etc. but I'm unique. No one has colorful flowers like mine or they just have one kind of that. I thank first, who created me & then, I thank you & your parents who planted me & other saplings, here."

The nightingale says unpassionately: "Is there any-thing else to talk about?"

The seven-colored flower: "Wow! I have many things to tell. I don't know how I should start or which one to express. You suggest a subject to talk about."

Other flowers are watching the seven-colored flower & the nightingale discussing. They understand the dispute between them. Because the seven-colored flower praised herself a lot & the nightingale was upset of that. The flowers decide not to join the discussion & just watch. An unknown flower who was covering herself says: "She's right. She's beautiful & everyone absorbed in her beauty." She stops & continues after a moment. It's an exciting discussion & it is worth to hear. As if the flower goes beyond the nightingale & the Dahlia says: "It's better to listen, but I think the seven-colored flower is right & she is going to succeed."

It's better to listen, but I think the seven- colored flower is right and she is going to succeed.

The other flowers just wait. As you saw, the 7-colred flower says her words and waits for the nightingale's speech. The mother's nightingale says: "I have a suggestion. Do you agree? Everybody accept. The father nightingale moves one of this wings to show his agreement and also the seven-colored flower raises branch. The mother nightingale: "I have a question from the seven-colored flower"

The seven-colored flower waits for the question and says: I'm ready to answer." She asks: why do you praise yourself this much while you should be praised?

The seven-colored flower surprises and understands that she had made a mistake.

Other flowers who got the nightingales point,

frown. The corn poppy says: "I don't let the seven-colored flower see her beauty and herself beyond us. The one who created us, knows what to do. So that we've got our right and there's no supremacy. We all should respect each other, be proud of anything we have and protect it." All the flowers shout: "Bravo, that's right."

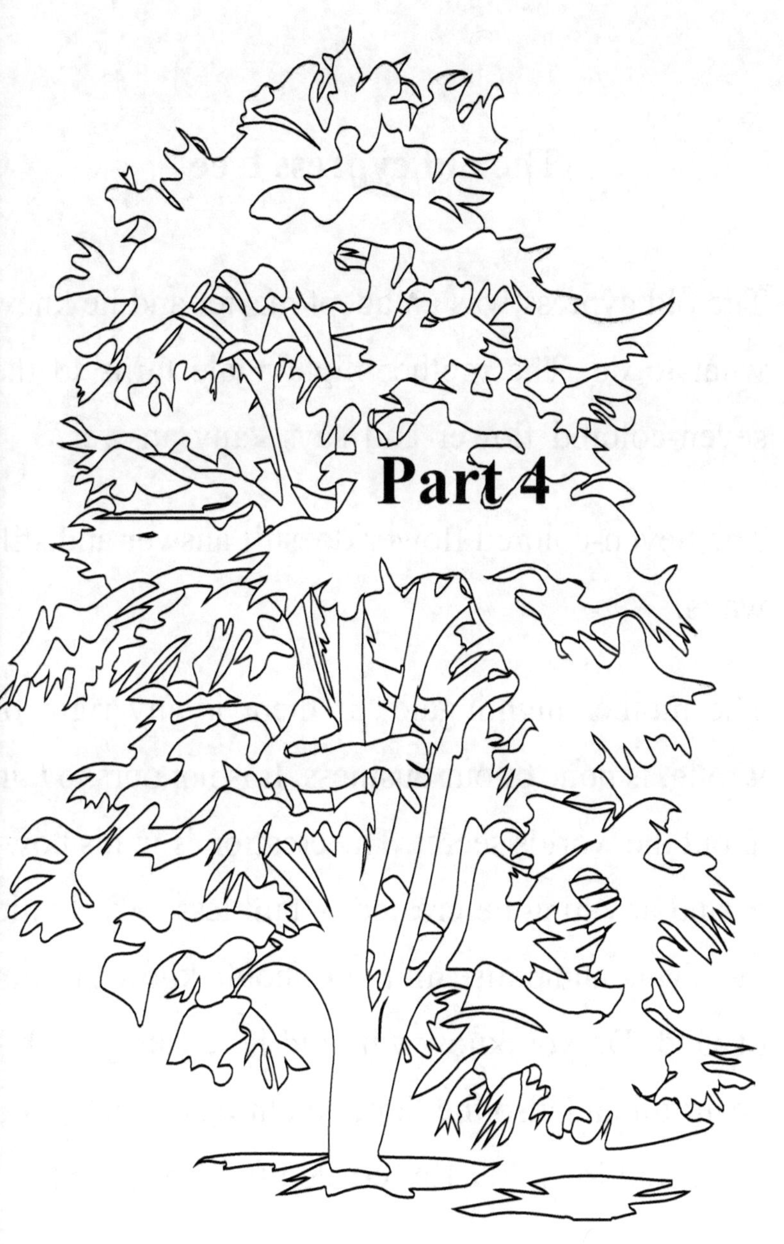

Part 4

The old cypress tree

The old cypress was an adept master and he knew what to do. The mother nightingale turns to the seven-colored flower and says "any answer?"

The Seven-colored flower doesn't answer and still waits.

The mother nightingale "if there is any right or wrong, is none of our business. It is not ours to talk about the worlds secret. The creation is in his power and anything he created is faultless. We should just thank and praise him. We should know the aim of God. Do you know why did he create you this beautiful and also the father nightingale: this good voice and lover but I'm created to be obedient?

Do you have any answer?

The seven-colored flower: I just said something without any discussion."

Corn poppy:" this discussion should be judged to be a lesson for other flowers. Do you agree?

Everybody confirms. The father nightingale says: the seven-colored flower is also agreed to be judged. "

The seven-colored flower: although I know that I'm right, I agree."

The father & mother nightingales whisper to each other.

The father nightingale: who is the greatest one in this island?"

The flowers answer "the old cypress. He is the old-est and he lives in the moon daisy

Flowers' quarter. He is clear-sighted in every prob-lem & we seek his advice."

The nightingale fly to that quarter & find the old cypress among the moon daisy. They sit on his branches, say hello and wait for his permission.

He starts to speak with them, answers their saluta-tion and asks them to tell what they want to.

He is a half-green tree and some parts of him are withered and effect. The nightingale defines the problem. The old cypress says: "I've just heard about your story from the rose flower and the moon daisy described you and your good voices for me. By the way, I answer you clearly. The 7- colored flower is more colorful than others without dept.

The dandelions all aware of the old cypress is speech and recite. The corn poppy is worried and frowned.

The old cypress continues: but no one must be ego-maniac in this island. No matter if you are more beautiful and taller. No one is superior to others. Just in case of being wise, theist and thankful of God, who created this island for us and our com-fort- the corn poppy becomes happy- we should be kind to each other and be friends . We've nev-er had such a discussion here and I hope to be the last one. But you, other flowers, you should be pa-tient. Don't' frown because God doesn't like it and the older of the island become worried. There are many good things to talk about. Now, the problem is solved and everyone knows his duty. I ask the father nightingale to sing, finish all the discussions, sing the "island's unity" song and I ask all of my friends to sing with the nightingale. Start."

Fine & beautiful flowers O'thou heart ravisher sing altogether sing altogether

If not being union not being integrity our world are annihilated and disgraced

Fine & beautiful flowers O'thou heart ravisher sing altogether sing altogether everyone

Union make pleasant make happiness otherwise it makes enemy

Fine & beautiful flowers O'thou heart ravisher sing altogether sing altogether

Union is support of life sing Union is motto of life if it is no there   enemy does damage

Fine & beautiful flowers O'thou heart ravisher sing altogether sing altogether

There's a stream beside the cypress. After finishing the song and the moon daisy's cheerfulness and happiness, another voice comes out of the stream who says: you, the old cypress!! Why do you stop singing?

Everybody turn to the voice and see an old turtle who has not seen yet. He is the old cypress tree's friend.

The cypress shouts: it's not finished yet. Come on my friend. Why did you keep me wait this long? Come on. I want to introduce you my friends."

The turtle approaches slowly and says: "what beautiful and nice friends! God is really kind to us.

Part 5

Old friend

In other part of the island and that region where the old cypress tree lives and the perspective of many colorful moon daisy, the wind makes the moon daisy touch each other and then, they sing a nice song together for the old cypress tree. He watches them happily, shares the happiness and comes along with them.

Moon daisy, manifest of happiness

Moon daisy, manifest of happiness

Our island brilliant and fine

our island like filigree

O' thou kind loving God

be flowers' helper

Moon daisy, manifest of happiness

Moon daisy, manifest of happiness

Always we say thank the truth, God

to be full of God's favor

This is the freeman's fame

this is the flowers' way of this district

Moon daisy, manifest of happiness

Moon daisy, manifest of happiness

The turtle comes:

God has given them a special beauty. Dear old cypress tree, I see that you become more powerful and cheerful every single day. I see it's because of these good friends and companions who entertain you.

The old cypress: you're right. There will be a lot of fun where there are good comates and neighbors.

The turtle: I don't stay here for a long. Say anything you want, because I don't want to fall behind my friends who are traveling want to impart your good memories and speeches.

The old cypress frowns and says: My friend! Why are you in hurry?

The old cypress has not finished his words yet that they hear the nightingale's voice. They land on a cypress's branch and say hello.

The old cypress says: hello my good friends... then, introducing them to the turtle: Dear turtle! These are my little new friends. Although they're little, they are excellent in thinking and singing. They impressed me. I want them to sing for you and you will see who they are.

The father nightingale: hello, good morning. I'm just here to say hello. I've just arrived and you ask me to sing, but I can't say No to the order one. They are apple of our eyes and they guide us. Now, I don't want to keep you waiting:

The mister taught me know the vows

Who planted love & kindness in all the existenc-es,

I found a place loving to sleep near the flower

Could not speak among the garden trees,

We watched unifying the flower with the friend

& we will be the sneeze to adorn the order,

We walked through this way to love Him forever

If the Mister thinks the hearts are in His way

All the flowers, specifically the moon daisy, the turtle and the old cypress tree rah. The nightingale embarrass and puts his wings on his eyes and stays in the position for a moment. It means thankfulness.

Everybody becomes quiet. The old cypress thanks everyone, too.

The turtle says: you are wholehearted in vow, juggle and happiness. This is the God's sweet favor. "I would stay here if my friends didn't wait for me."

The flowers look at each other and smile. The old

cypress says: you are always welcome, here is belonged to everyone. You see that we enjoy God's favor and kindness and we are thankful. Try to come sooner next year and stay with us for a while.

****

The 7 colored flower sends a message by the Dandelion including these words: I can see some movements in the ocean. Something is happening there. Although the ocean is not stormy, the water moves.

Yes. They are the turtle's friends. He says: I should go. My friends become worried. He says goodbye to all with tearful eyes and moves away slowly.

The old cypress asks all to the convoy him with a song:

"Welcome to the island, our little friend,

You are welcomed, happy our friendship"

Finally the turtle arrives to the water, turns his head, looks back and then disappears.

The old cypress tells the nightingales:" waiting is finished, but you, my good friends welcome to this island."

The nightingales thanks him and flowers. They promise to meet them again and to sing the friendship song:

"Welcome to the island, our little friends,

You are welcomed, happy our friendship"

The nightingales say goodbye, fly over the cypress tree and moon daisy, sing and dance. Then they move away and enjoy the flowers dance.

Part 6

Deep freezing

The nightingales are sitting on the 7 colored flowers branch in this spring morning and a fresh breeze, they get up, open their wings and clap and say "good morning" to each other. The seven -colored flower gets upset because they didn't say hello to her and complains to them. The little good -voiced birds says hello to her nervously.

The seven -colored flower smiles with a satisfactory and answers their solution.

The mother nightingale dresses up herself and performs her features with the seven -colored flower. The father nightingale starts singing and attracts the attention of the island's habitants to himself and the 7_colored flowers:

O'Thou God gave a good shape to flowers

I became ravish of world creation

Love and ravishing are shined from every flower
the ravisher's heart is burned from this love fire

Morning breeze and nightingale's song is merited
to be heard with flower dancing

The nightingale stops singing. The corn poppy and
other flowers complain and ask him to sing. The
nightingale says:" Morning flight, exercising with
the flowers, smell, clean air, fly to the aim." Then
he disappears in other come along with her, dance
and exercise together:

Wake up flowers to play

It's time for our happiness,

We exercise everyday

Getting along the sneeze day,

Sometimes to right, sometimes to left

Only we dance with the sneeze,

Wake up flowers to play

It's time for our happiness

They are still dancing.

This time, the nightingales go to an alone and departed tree. They sit on his branch. The tree is very old, it is obvious from his thick body and time worn branches. The father nightingale says hello to him.

The tree was napping. He opens his eyes. The nightingale says gracefully:" excuse me that I wake you up".

The tree: "No problem. What a little bird. Here was full of the birds like you in the past. I don't know why they disappeared and left here suddenly."

The nightingale asks about his loneliness. The tree says:" it's because of mischance and he starts speaking about the past memories and experiences. "Now, I don't know where these new flowers and trees come from. The island is full of flowers now. I see them from this distance and enjoy."

The nightingale:" so you have lots of memories from here, right? I ask you to introduce yourself." The pine tree introduces himself and says:" There is a tree called "the old cypress". He is a member of our family and he lives in the moon daisy region. Send my regards if you meet him.

His father and I were friends, but he died, then these branches grew. It grew, but withered by a long tide again. Most of these flowers whiter and their seeds grow again, because too much water is not good for the flowers. It makes them become pale and weak."

The nightingale looks at his partner sadly, because the tree is so alone.

They are whispering:" we should come to him sometimes and speak with him."

The pine tree can't understand their talking and he asks: "what are you talking about?"

The nightingale says:" Don't be sad. We didn't tell bad things. I was consulting with my wife about coming to you, so you won't be alone anymore...

The pine tree laughs:" you could say it loudly. By the way, thank you."

Then he becomes quiet. It seems he's thinking. Suddenly, he startles and says:" you might have good voices. The birds.... you were good -voiced before. "

 How do you know I'm good-voiced, too?

I had a lot of contacts with birds when I was young. When that freezing cold came, many birds, flowers and thin trees withered and the others left here and never came back. "

The nightingale understands the reason that no bird or animal live here and asks the pine tree to tell them more memories. The pine tree says:" we have a lot of time and many things to say. But the memories of the past are sad. Don't hurry.

Sing for me. I'm upset, for telling about the past you should be alone."

The nightingale says:" No problem. It's a little late, today. I should go to my friends, too. Because they'll become worried."

The pine tree:" so you don't sing for me?"

The nightingale:" No, my friend sing. Listen please. I wish you won't become sad and stars:

My heart is broken of loneliness

My heart is getting old of loneliness,

What if God forget about me?

What if he didn't compromise with me?

Thank you from bottom of my heart

I try to praise you every moment,

Time to leave, Goodbye

Come back soon, goodbye

Then he moves far from that area and comes back
to the nest.

part 7

The olive tree's memories

The pine tree waits for his little friends. He rises his branches and looks at far away. Looks at the way that they come and went from, yesterday.

He speaks with himself:" they don't come. "What cute friends" suddenly, he hears their voices from his back. He says:" you came from that way yesterday. I was looking for you there."

The nightingales say hello and the pine tree answers:" he look very happy. The father nightingale says:" I'm so willing to listen to your memories. I'm really interested in the past of you and island.

My wife and I are ready to listen to your words and

news."

The pine tree says:" why are you in hurry this much? Do you think that our spring is finished and it that the reason of your impatience? We are together and we have a lot of time. Sing a little for me. Then I tell you one of my untold memories."

The nightingale says:" alright. I sing, but I want the best memories of you."

_ of course, sing sweet heart:

If you want to know the secret old knowledge

You should suffer the pain,

Everyone who searched & found

Heard the history from the school's heart,

Learn the lesson of life

Spend the life for learning,

Mother of world is our Mister

Who teaches us the ancient destiny

The pine tree becomes full of happiness. he says:" Bravo, Bravo, that was great." for many times and continues, but I don't Know whether you like these memories or you pass from them!"

The father nightingale says: tell whatever be bitter or sweet it should be hearable we are ready to hear.

Ok. So listen, that from a friend in the name of olive tree who told me this memory.

Once a ship come here. The ship broke down, so cut the olive tree and repair the ship and her want. Now, the roots of that olive tree budded and grew up but nobody knows this venture even the pine tree. One day morning which the sun rose to shine everywhere. Bud of olive tree called me and said look at me, I turn to the voice. I saw our small island was fried. A frightening voice from burnt place came to my ear. The earth was shaken. Firm shakes spoke us.

We were afraid. The olive tree said: this island came out of water and were built. I asked now what's happen. It answered fire goes out of the earth. The men of ship who repaired their ship said the volcano deep under the Sea erupted, we should move as soon as possible and then they went.

First, this island was very small then after erupting this island became big but the story here is tragic. The lava erupted from the crater and covered the island. All flowers and polts were burnt and annihilated. That fire was blown out and the time passed little by little other flowers grew up and reside all the island.

Every survived birds brought the seeds and spores of the plants from the near island to this island. Then they planted them. Now you can see that every parts of the island is full of colorful flowers and we see there are a lot of beautiful flowers in a region. It's because of bringing that seeds. I saw this events 80 years ago, but the olive tree was 700 years old. I wish he could grow again and refund our first happiness. You are my good friends and if the olive tree was a live, I would introduce you to him."

The nightingale:" Maybe he can grow again. We haven't checked carefully."

He stands up and flies to the place the pine tree shows. He sits on the cut body of the olive tree and starts checking. Suddenly he sees a little sapling and shouts with smile:" there's a sapling."

The mother nightingale comes and looks carefully. The sapling laughs and says:" tell the pine tree that where there is a wish, there is a way. I'll grow soon and we'll be the friends."

The pine tree laughs, then he cries. He remembers the ship of two feet humans destroyed, they picked up all of the olive trees fruit and then shattered him."

A fluent voice transfix the nightingales and the pine tree. They pay attention and understand that the olive trees sapling is singing:

I'm young, happy, singing, want to grow

I'm singing, knowing, want to have thousand years,

 Hey you sea, hey you flowers, I want to grow

We're together, singing together, I want to be beautiful,

Hey island, hey island, we should make you beautiful

We're happy, we are young, making the world beautiful

Lalala lalala lalala lalala…

Also the pine tree rejoiced. The nightingale flew from this branch to another branch. Also the mother nightingale joined them to make merry. The nightingale says, by the way, the cypress tree said hello. Now that I leave you I tell about your happiness.

All habitant of the island should become glad.

The pine tree became gladder because his massage has come to the old cypress tree. Nightingales were going to say goodbye and fly. It seems that in some pants on the island as if the blood is flowing and rippling. All are red corn pappy dancing and singing.

The mother nightingale says you promise seven color flower that you will come back very soon. What reason you have!

The pine tree gaily tells himself I don't know why the olive tree budded two or three times then withered. I should request the nightingale that ask the old cypress tree about the reason to solve the problem. Sing again the olive bud. Sing my dear!

part8

Visiting corn poppy

The nightingale and his spouse, on the morning, are sleep while their head are below their wings. Little by little the sun rises and shines

The earth. The song of be ready is played and this is done by lilies. The day arrives it's the time of wake up. The father nightingale wakes up and look at around, shake his wings, calls his couple and says: rose, my dear rose its morning get up everyone are waked up. The female nightingale see herself on the hoarfrost make up herself.

Then she stroke a few sweet-smelling flowers and came back to her nest to be prepared to go to region of the Corn poppies. All flowers are dancing while

breeze streaming and morning exercise and created
a happy and merry situation, all are singing:

Hey you flowers, nightingales, stand up

The sun is back, everyone should stand up,

The darkness is gone from us

The sun is back, everyone should stand up,

Stand up, stand up

Stand up, stand up

Morning exercise was ended and the couple nightingale fly to place where the corn poppies are there.

The seven color flower says loudly: my dears come
back soon,

Don't keep me waiting. The father nightingale turns

and says: of, then they go far. He see far the region of corn poppies full of different colors.

I said it seems like a sea of blood.

Their tumult and song are heard. Blossom like children of men in the adults, bosom shake and steal away heart. It seems that the older kiss their beautiful faces.

The nightingales are going to sit on their branch that the mother nightingale says: wait let them be glad. We also please with them.one of corn poppers sees them. Hey, hey I call you.

Oh beautiful bird come and dance with us. The father nightingale say wanted not to spoil your fun and we enjoy behind you.

The beautiful corn poppy scowled and sadly said,

no, no l don't think you want to spoil our fun. Listen and look, all sing a song in harmony. The nightingales are happily and excitedly sing together:

Red poppy corn flower like bride wear colored velvets

Beautiful flower is not forever long

friends' memory is not forgettable, dears

If you see corn poppy's tear

see double- fine eyes

You be charmed from the truth creatures   you write many about their world

The father nightingale who see that happiness become impatient land on a branch and delicately twitters and sings. All flowers become silent. All corn poppies sing too. Again the breeze starts to blow.

Flowers kiss together. Whatever they steal away heart, the and double love and passion:

You made me happy by your coquettish songs

You made me fall in love with you all,

Do I deserve to fall in love?

Do I deserve to know the flowers secrets?

The nightingale couple came to the flower and sit and sees himself in hoarfrost, and again strokes herself to flowers. A few corn poppies surround her and in a beautiful manner in clip mother nightin-gale.

The father nightingale sees his couple under corn

poppies garland again sings:

Ho! Beauties! What did have you done to us?

You attracted all the world to us,

If I'm astonished & impatient

You've made me insane, didn't you?

He gives a kiss flowers and his partner. Corn puppies shoot the mother nightingale toward the father nightingale and she sits behind him. A group of corn poppies say in harmonic, beautiful birds welcome to us. All cheer and cry for Joy, the father nightingale says: Not to embrace us. Your favors have tied my tongue.

He prays God. Oh my god Not to withdraw this glad and excitement. All says Amen. She asked him to go now, the seven colors flower becomes worried. He feels that she is jealous, because the father nightingale did them a kindness. He understands her feeling and says: how you want to isolate a frenzied nightingale from flowers? Like a believer who warship. This is our truth.

Flowers should be fondle, we should recite God to reach the nature which is the same belief and faith.

The object of writing stories in human language is that all life of human and animals are on the hands of God.so whatever we need to prepare is on the hands if God and the best relation is relation with the Almighty God creates brings up and takes human's life and life pass that its helm is on the hands of God. Thanks God who those who pray always God and be far from oppression and cruelty and replace kindness by unfair and disorder are successful

in both world, after word and whatever they want
God, he provide for them and set free pressure and
poverty and those who select one but God and obey
Devil offers hard in both world and after worlds, I
hope that we be of the best. God wishes.

part 9

Festival of the flower becoming one year old

It's a spring morning. All are happy. Flowers are talking to each other mincingly. Suddenly lilies sound reverberates on the region all become silent. No sound is heard. Where are those cheers? Says Good morning and ask them pay attention. Some of one year flower buds little by little and again grow up.

Different seeds, spores and bulbs start new life then we lost them.

It is their fate and they live for one year. They are happy and satisfied with it. they withered little by little to prepare the situation for seeds etc. then come back to life again today, we are witness their one year Festival or more or less.

They all enjoyed enough. Our life is like this and we adjust with it. Each of them in proportion His/her status of love for this reason we hold this festival one month before because no one missed. Our being is beauty and our absence is memory which each of us is going to stay in this world and is not forgettable. Many years this ceremony was hold and has been hold. Because every creature review these memories and joys and fight against unpleasantness so that with happily living and hope we pass memory. Now I ask all beautiful habitants of the island to sing a song specific for this day, so let's start:

We come to make good memories,

We go together happily

The honor is ours,

To devote our life to life

How sweet it is that,

I put this life in your hand

Buds walking with a long skirt touching the
ground,

Our mother speaks masterfully

Today dew gives out buttercup smell,

With hundred words from shining world

Nymphs with faces like moon all rejoicing,

Time comes back again welcome again

We who don't remain unaware of happy song,

Shine with breeze of dance

We are flower-face, well-spoken, mystic,

Next year we are together again

Each of us goes to sweet sleep more quickly,

Our name, your name is recalled nicely every day

One who brought us to life will take us back again   someday,

Finally others will take a departure too,

They came happy and leaves hardly

Let out happy cry   sing a happy song   time of expressing your joy

My dear read a sonnet darling   say the words of song my desting   lose your heart happily   all you are ravished with pride   how beauty and lovely you are Flower and nightingale with happy

Island my home

all you are heart-stealer

All you are ravished from honor

what a beautiful and mignon

Flower and nightingale are happy

With the nightingale's point everybody remained silent. All wait to see what he says then the nightingale reads a beautiful poem.

We are all well-spoken & pure-hearted,

We all give up our ghost

Days pass and we are alive,

We all die for sweethearts

End point of each person is one of these days,

Everybody clap and accepts that everybody is enti-
tled to be revived and return. Nightingales fly and
again the island like beachcomber dance and sing.

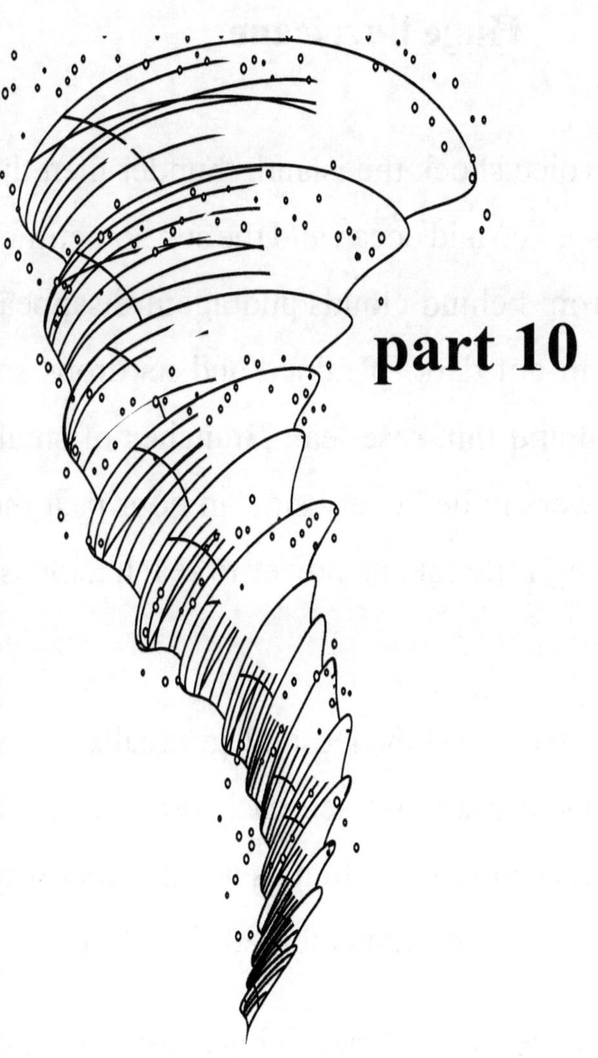

part 10

Huge hurricane

A horrible voice shock the island, thunder then the island was shaken and ocean and the sun sometimes appeared from behind clouds and again disappear and the earth got dark. It rained and its drops sat on beautiful and thin rose leaf. Branches of small and big flowers pulled every side an hour past the storm little by little lots its power to reach a pleasant breeze.

All flowers were disheveled and gradually stand with blowing breeze and see each other. After a while all stand on this position as usual sometimes smile and sometimes remembered the storm.

The Nightingales spread their wings under the sun

light to dry, then Flies, go back to their beautiful friend and be aware of their status. Lilies blow in its trumpet, the dandelions flied to send their message and said the island is safe.

Everyone did its duty to provide friends and island with comfort. All sought each other. Seven color flowers' leaves shined from far distance as if in its leaves it had glitter and its flowers show beauty and freshness. The seven color flower ask the nightingale to sing and change the atmosphere in order to forget storm and dance. The nightingale said: ok my beautiful flower. I fly round to take news then come back to sing. The Nightingale flew. He saw the island from up then he sat on a branch of seven-colored flower then start to sing.

two crowns sang loudly everybody look around croak, croak is not there any big tree we go there to land on it everywhere is full of flowers and plants to sit, go toward trees. Then they goes far.

For a moment their calmness was broken, again a noise was heard. A thin sound of the marigold tinkled in the air. She said:" my dear flowers, good-smelled plants and beautiful Nightingales of this island! I want to talk to you. Then I sing a poem perhaps you enjoy. Do you let me?" All cry out "Hurrah" and encourage it:" I found that the storm was over. Rain washed everywhere. The storm removed dust to the depth of ocean. The crowns' sound that seemed bad mood were heard morning song and dance of the Nightingale was heard all enjoyed and frightened and became calm. Nevertheless all we must try to make our island beautiful. Don't waste time. Everybody should do anything to make fun of each other. We should be positive. I said a poem. Let me read it, it is all my power that you hear.":

End point of each person is one of these days, All of the flowers sing to encourage the marigold flower:

The poet marigold is   better than us.

The smart marigold   what a handsome

The marigold thanks everyone.

part 11

The Pine tree

The old tree talk about the pine tree and points him to the others. He asks him to tell them a memory about the creation of the island, its dusting and the volcano which made the island.

The pine tree is very burly and it can be considered of his body that he lived long, but today he is cut and burned and what remains has not grown allot. Nevertheless he is not withered. He says: This Island has created because of the volcano. It wasn't this beautiful, but little by little the growth began. so that the salesman of the ships who were passing from the ocean, got off here and sometimes they stayed for a long time. All that live, they brought some shrubs to plant such as me, the old olive tree, the cypress tree and many of the flowers.

After a while, the marigold island become so beautiful that there were no island as beautiful as here.
Many kinds of birds outbreed and made nests.
There were an indescribable rumpus. God wishes to
everyone having no bad day. Suddenly the ground
disported in an early morning, the stones and ashes
were thrown to the air and everywhere was full of
smoke. The island was covered by the lava. The
birds who had chickens or eggs, run away or some
of them burned. After some days the smoke disappeared and the air became fleshed.

The birds came back to find their burned chickens
and eggs. They couldn't find them. They just fly to
the near island sadly. After a while, they brought
some flowers and seeds to put on their chicken
graves. They planted them and the previous beauty

of the island came back. I wish such events won't happen again.

Because it's a dark events and it takes many years to reborn.

The flowers by listening to that story, begin to sing for the memory of the pasts and they ask God that such things won't happen again. It's such a pity with this kind of beauty!? They all sing together:

Time! Compromise with us!

Send your blessings to us,

With your compromise & kindness

Give us the honor, you our Judge,

Our Creator is our hope

We are frenzied with His love,

You gave us our life mercifully

You gave us your kindness cheerfully,

Our calmness is from our love

You are the Giver, you send your kindness,

We thank you every moment

You give us the honor flourishingly

Of this time, the nightingale arrives and the night bumming jasmine flower, tells him the pine tree told story about the past. The nightingale becomes sad and sings:

Hey! You who pass the past! Cheer to you

We spent here, listening your story,

Our mothers' heart are broken

We cry out for that broken ones,

We get no treats with this clamor

It'll pas but we have no fortitude,

We are astonished, we'll be astonished

Every year, there's a favor for us

Now, the olive tree wants to speak as a witness of that disaster. He says: dear flowers, be aware that we all are mortal. The old pine tree told us that memory and reminded us that disaster. It is passed, but we should know and believe that the history is full of such happenings. It's better not to talk about. Talk about the present and future. Be happy in order not to get withered. Every creatures are mortal and they die one day. So, don't waste the time of happiness. Appreciate the presence. We come and go. The GOD watches us. The island and the creatures are mortal.

So try to enjoy the moment. I wish you be successful and more beautiful than the past and your good
memories won the bad ones. Thank you.

Everybody gets ready for the ending song to finish
the conversations happily:

**The flower time arrives, the spring is here so
welcomed**

**We get crazy of love, truly yours, welcome the
spring,**

We are beautiful, we sing the bests

We get the harmony of time, we get lesson of life,

We are the God's kindness lovers & thankful

We walk through the time, we enjoy our life,

**Astonished forever, they've written many things
of us**

But we made this pen is his hand unwritten able,

Goodbye all you dears reading our story

We've heard & seen, getting calmness,

The flower time arrives, the spring is here so welcomed

We get crazy of love, truly yours, welcome the
spring